The World's Greatest Composers

Bob Marley

by Marsha Bronson

Picture Credits:
Adrian Boot: 4 (bottom), 8-9 (main picture), 9 (bottom inset), 13 ,15, 16, 17, 18, 23, 27 (above), 29, 30, 31, 33, 35, 36, 44, 50, 54; Bridgeman Art Library: 26 (bottom); Chris Corr: 58; Gamma Presse: 3 (above), 5, 9, (top inset), 11, 27 (bottom), 45, 51, 59; London Features International: 19, cover; Popperfoto: 6, 21, 25, 47, 52; David Redfern: 40-1, 48 (below); Rex Features: 48 (above), 55; United Nations (WHO): 12 (top inset); Zefa: 12 (bottom), 26 (above), 56.

Lyrics used by permission of
BOB MARLEY MUSIC LTD /
BLUE MOUNTAIN MUSIC LTD.
"Get Up, Stand Up" © 1973, Cayman
Music Inc / Stuck on Music, USA.
Reproduced (in the British
Commonwealth and Eire) by
permission of Cayman Music Inc /
EMI Tunes Plc, London
WC2H 0EA, UK.
Photocopying the above copyright
material is illegal.

Published in Great Britain in 1993
by Exley Publications Ltd,
16 Chalk Hill, Watford,
Herts WD1 4BN, United Kingdom.

Copyright © Exley Publications, 1993
Copyright © Marsha Bronson, 1993

A copy of the CIP data is available from
the British Library on request

ISBN 1-85015-312-4

Series editor: Helen Exley
Editor: Samantha Armstrong
Picture editors: Alex Goldberg and James
Clift of Image Select
Editing: Margaret Montgomery
Typeset by Delta Print, Watford, UK
Printed and bound in Hungary

Bob
MARLEY

by Marsha Bronson

⧓EXLEY

Above: Kingston, Jamaica: the Trenchtown district in the run-up to the 1979 elections was a dangerous place to be. A contract killer, or "Yardie", could be hired to murder a political rival for ten dollars.
Right: Painted on a wall, the scene Jamaica will never forget. Bob Marley persuaded the bitterly-opposed political leaders to join their hands in a gesture of peace.

One peace

If there is one moment that Jamaica will never forget, it is a moment on the stage of the country's National Stadium in 1978, Bob Marley held aloft and clenched above his head the hands of the country's two rival political leaders - Edward Seaga and Michael Manley. In the background, the leaders of Jamaica's two rival gangs embraced each other.

This moment electrified the crowd in the stadium. It electrified every Jamaican at home and abroad. It was captured by the world's cameras and went down in history as a moment of triumph for Jamaica, and for Bob Marley, its most famous son.

The reconciliation of Jamaica's most bitter rivals took place during the twelve-hour marathon "One Love One Peace" concert, organized to celebrate the newly-signed peace treaty between the two political parties. The treaty and concert were the idea of a leading member of the Jamaican Labour Party, Claude Massop, who had joined forces with a member of the opposing People's National Party, Bucky Marshall. Both Massop and Marshall realized that no celebration would be possible without Jamaica's hero: music legend, Rastafarian, and reggae's greatest star, Bob Marley.

Marley was returning to his island home after an absence of two years, and he found Jamaica in a state of great turmoil. Racked by violence and poverty, it was overrun by gangs who fought their private battles on the public streets. Little had changed since the days he was growing up in the Kingston slums. One of his first singles ever, "Simmer Down", released in 1964, had been a plea for peace among Kingston's gang rivals. "In Jamaica you're expected to use your knife, or your machete, or your gun," he lamented. In 1976, he himself had fallen victim to the gun: he was the first, but sadly not the last, musical star in Jamaica to suffer an assassination attempt. But he survived, and continued with even greater zeal to release albums that told the world about his oppressed countrymen.

Members of the Jamaicain drug mafia pose with their guns. After the violence surrounding the 1979 election, many of the Kingston gunmen emigrated to Miami and were killed in battles with drug gangs there. Now, posters around Kingston use pictures of Bob Marley to urge young people, "Just say No drugs and guns."

A history of struggle

The slave trade: throughout the colonization of the West Indies by the Europeans, African Negroes were imported from Angola and sold as slaves when the native populations resisted, or died of European diseases. The slave trade continued well into the nineteenth century, with slaves being sold by public auction in town squares. This history of captivity formed the theme of many of Marley's songs, such as "Redemption Song" and "Slave Driver".

Bob Marley was born in the village of Nine Miles in 1945 in the poor, hilly parish of St. Ann. But the struggle he became involved in began a long time before that. In fact, it is possible to trace the history of his oppressed people right back to the end of the fifteenth century, when a Spanish ship sailed into Dry Harbour, along the north coast of Jamaica, then inhabited by the Arawak Indians.

The year was 1496, and the ship's captain was Christopher Columbus - the first white person ever to set foot on the Caribbean island.

The Spanish made slaves of the Arawak Indians, many of whom died of European diseases. Still more of the Indians committed suicide, the idea of slavery more terrible to them than the idea of death. Undeterred, the Spanish imported slaves from Angola, on the south western coast of Africa. These Africans are the direct ancestors of today's black Jamaicans.

The British invaded Jamaica in the middle of the seventeenth century, taking the island by force from the Spanish. This was in 1655, and five years later the British drew up a treaty to make the island officially theirs. They were bitterly opposed by the Jamaican slaves, descendants of the imported Angolans, who fled to the hills and waged guerrilla war on the British. These guerrillas were so violent and reckless that they became known as "Maroons", from the Spanish word *marrano,* which means "unruly".

So, the islands of the Caribbean were destroyed and re-created by a stream of European invaders: the Dutch, the British, the Portuguese, the Spanish and the French. The entire West Indies stretches from Cuba, just ninety miles from the United States, to Trinidad, close to the Venezuelan coast of South America. Like a crooked bridge linking North and South America, the islands are a product of great turmoil and a rich mixture of cultures and traditions.

In Jamaica itself, slavery only ended in 1834. British missionaries then helped the freed slaves to build "free" villages and begin the long recovery from over three hundred years of slavery. Some of the earliest of these villages were in the parish of Bob Marley's birthplace, St. Ann, around the hills and valleys of Eight Miles and Nine Miles.

The Malcolms and the Marleys

Bob's grandfather on his mother's side, Omeriah Malcolm, was a short man, and he was a person who commanded great respect in the community. He was a very popular man, and was often known simply and affectionately as "O.M.". He was a hard-working and clean-living man, who farmed the land around Nine Miles. His wife was Alberta (Yaya) Wilby.

Bob's father, Captain Norval Marley, was from a white Jamaican family. He was a quartermaster with the British East Indian regiment, and looked after the land around a village called Rhoden Hall. He first met and fell in love with Bob's mother, Cedella, when he was almost fifty years old and she was just eighteen.

Omeriah Malcolm was furious when his young daughter told him she was carrying the child of a

Captain in the British army, and moreover, a member of the Marley family. The Marleys were known to "disapprove" of blacks, and Omeriah feared for his daughter's future. However, he relented when Norval Marley rode out to his farm to ask him in person for Cedella's hand in marriage.

Norval and Cedella were married on June 9, 1944. The marriage caused Captain Marley to be disinherited by his angry family. Very soon after the wedding, he left to work in Kingston.

Bob Marley was born on February 6 the following year, in the parish of St. Ann. Known as "the garden parish", it was one of the most fertile and productive areas of Jamaica. It was also the spiritual heart of the island. "I come from country and country is always good," Bob was always saying. "You grow everything."

His name, like the warm brown of his skin, was evidence of the mix of races and influences that make up Jamaica's rich and exciting culture. He was named Robert after his father's brother, an influence from

Main picture: The third largest island in the Caribbean, Jamaica's hot climate, about 80°F all year round, and annual rains make for lush vegetation, which is ideal for crops such as sugar, coffee and bananas.

Top: The house where Bob Marley spent the early years of his life, in the village of Nine Miles – so called because it was nine miles from St. Ann's Bay.

Below: In stark contrast to Bob's tin-roofed early home, the wealthy whites of Kingston lived comfortably. At the height of his fame, Bob lived in a big house on Hope Road, but his only luxury was a BMW car. It is estimated that he supported four thousand of Jamaica's poor by sharing Rastafari stew and rice with anyone who his house.

white Jamaica. But his middle name, Nesta, was chosen by his mother, a black Jamaican.

Cedella and Norval's romance sounds like a fairy tale, because he was willing to resist the opposition of his family and the taboos of society to marry her. But, sadly, the couple did not live happily ever after. Norval spent most of the time away and Bob was without a real father from the age of six.

Cedella always spoke fondly of her first husband, she knew him to be a good man with the best intentions. But, Bob himself expressed anger over his father's treatment of them. "I think my father was a bad man," he said.

Nevertheless, his confused beginnings actually helped to cultivate the mystique that would later surround him. Such a mystique was extremely valuable to a man who was to present so many different sides of himself to the world. No one ever seemed to have a full picture of Marley the man. No one was fully sure where he had come from (he led people to believe that he and his family came from Africa), and this mysterious aspect of him added to the myths and legends that grew up around him. Some said he was a prophet, others an emissary from Jah (the Rasta god). But everyone realized that he was special, someone capable of bringing awareness to the oppressed people of Jamaica.

The palm reader

During Bob's childhood, there were several instances when the people around him felt he had special gifts. As a small boy, he sometimes predicted the future by reading people's palms. Several times, friends came to Cedella and told her "That boy has a real gift - he told me what would happen and he was right."

Bob's palm reading stopped when Cedella received a letter from her husband telling her that he wanted his son to attend school in Kingston town. Unwilling to lose her little boy to the unknown dangers of the capital, Cedella watched him go with tears in her eyes. After he went, she tried hard to keep in contact with her husband and get regular news of her son, but she didn't hear anything for a whole year.

One day, a friend returning from Kingston told Cedella she had seen Bob playing in the yard of an old woman in the city. He had told her he was not going to school at all, but living with the old lady, and that his father had left him there. Frightened and confused, Cedella set out for Kingston. She found the seven-year-old Bob at the home of a rich, but ailing, old woman, Mrs. Grey, whom Norval had hoped would leave the boy some of her money.

Cedella was angry, and determined that Bob should come back home with her. So Bob returned to St. Ann's. He seemed unharmed by his experience in the city, and he had a new interest: he began to sing. He accompanied himself on his first ever guitar, made for him by his cousin, Nehemiah, out of a herring pan, with strings attached to a wooden fretwork. Cedella, a deeply religious woman, was often singing spiritual songs around the house. Much later Bob told her that, whenever he sang, he felt the same way that she had when she sang and "got into the spirit".

Bob's mother, Cedella Booker, known in Jamaica as "Mother B". She first saw her son perform in Philadelphia in 1970. "Him say to me, when him singing him feel the same way like when I was singing in church when I go into the spirit ... If he say him feel like me, then he must really feel good."

11

Below: The two faces of Kingston: Trenchtown, a ghetto of poverty and disease, where no tourist is ever taken or dares to go; bottom, the modern, wealthy side of Kingston the tourists see.
Opposite: music provides the bond that draws together the multi-racial children of Jamaican schools.

Started out crying

Many years later, an interviewer asked the famous reggae star: "Bob, how did you start out in singing?"

"Started out ... crying," replied Marley. "Yeah, started out crying."

Bob was raised in poverty. His father died in 1955, and later that year, Cedella moved to the capital to find work. This time, she left Bob in safe hands, looking after the goats on his grandfather's farm. He attended a series of schools, and for a while lived with his tyrannical Aunt Amy, where Omeriah sent him and his cousin, Sledger. However, the two boys soon escaped and came running back to their grandad. It was a streak of rebellion that Bob developed to sustain him during his bewildering childhood.

In 1957, Cedella finally had enough money saved to send for her son. For the second time, Bob went to live in Kingston, and a new stage of his life began. He came to know the slums of Kingston as well as he knew the small farms and basic lifestyle of St. Ann.

Kingston 12

In the squatter settlements of Kingston 12, the government-built high-rise flats, at least eight people lived together in a room that measured seven by ten feet. There were communal "yards" where whole families shared cooking and sanitary facilities. They were full of poor farmers who could no longer afford to keep up their farms and had to move to Kingston in search of work, bringing their families with them. Conditions in these yards bred diseases, like typhoid fever and polio.

The people in Kingston 12 were known as "sufferahs" or "Israelites", because they identified with the disinherited tribes from the Bible's Old Testament. But they also had a spirit of great defiance, of rebellion against the systems that put them in this position of poverty.

Places like Trenchtown, which was built over a sewage ditch that drained Old Kingston, and the so-called Concrete Jungle, like Kingston 12, were home to a whole new movement called the "Rude Boys". Rudies, or Rude Boys, were young men, aged between fourteen and thirty, who moved from the rural areas to the town in the 1960s. When they couldn't find work, they turned living on the streets into their careers. They stood for rebellion against authority, for protest and for rage.

The image of Rude Boy is closely bound up with the Kingston term, "dread". Dread signifies a spiritual strength, a willingness to oppose oppressive authority; to try, and - most importantly - to endure failure and hardship with strength.

Judge Dread

The Rude Boys invented a judge, whom they called Judge Dread. He was harsh and unjust, and was said by the Rude Boys to hand out sentences of more than a thousand years. Judge Dread is a symbol for the powerful ruling classes, because a judge is also in power, and able to control people's lives with a single decision. The Rude Boys felt their rulers, like Judge Dread, were without mercy or fairness, and would stop at nothing to remain in power.

Judge Dread's imaginary long sentences corresponded to all the real agonies suffered by the Arawak Indians, the black slaves imported from Africa, and their true Jamaican descendants, bound in the shackles of their European masters. Thus, the Rude Boys created a character on whom they could vent their anger at the hundreds of years their ancestors had suffered as slaves.

Bob Marley knew all about his roots in such suffering. He had heard stories about the slaves and the humiliation they suffered at the hands of their European masters. And while such stories nourished in him a reverence for his roots, they also stirred in him the Rude Boy rage of protest against injustice.

"Tuff Gong"

For Bob, life in Kingston was a scattered and disjointed affair. He finished school in 1960, at the age of fifteen, and started to learn welding in a workshop. He hated welding, but there was always the much more important business of music.

Luckily, his job provided him with a vital contact who was to help him sow the seeds of his musical career: Desmond Dekker.

That year, Dekker and the Aces had released "The Israelites", the first Jamaican song to be a hit in the European charts. Dekker introduced Marley to Jimmy Cliff, who in turn helped the fifteen-year-old Bob Marley to get his first song on record. It was called "Judge Not". It wasn't until Bob was wandering home with the record under his arm that he realized he didn't have a player to play it on.

Late in 1960, Bob's mother moved to the United States, where she was married within a year to a civil servant named Edward Booker. Bob and his young half-sister Pearl stayed with their Aunt in Kingston. After she married, Cedella returned to Kingston to collect Bob and Pearl, but Bob, now sixteen, preferred to stay there and make his music.

In Kingston, Bob learned to be tough. He often stayed with friends and distant relatives, and soon earned the nickname "Tuff Gong". As one of his biographers said: "Bob Marley was at many times an

1964: Bob, aged nineteen, was so poor he relied on producer Clement Dodd to provide him with stage clothes, like this tight-fitting black suit and these pointed shoes.

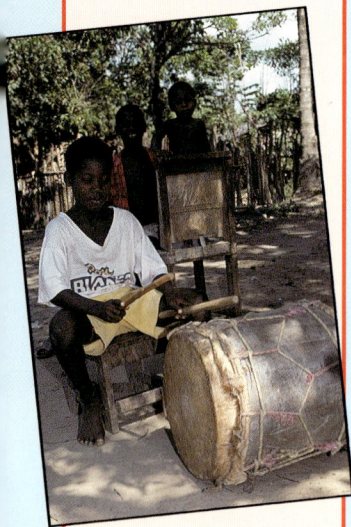

Above and right: The South American drum and the Caribbean steel band – the drum rhythm is at the heart of black music. Rastafarians took over the ancient Afro-Jamaican style of drumming known as "burru". Originally, burru's heart-beat rhythm was used to celebrate the liberation of Jamaican prisoners and welcome them back to their villages.
Right: the Jamaican music that Bob would have heard in his childhood was made out of bamboo and gourds.

abandoned child; and this condition was a key to his poetic sensibility."

In the backyards of the Kingston slums, he played guitar with his friends - Bunny (Neville) Livingston and Pete Tosh (Winston McIntosh). These early friendships, bonds sealed by the love of music and the need to play, were to form the basis for the most famous band in reggae history: Bob Marley and the Wailers.

Garden-boy music

Reggae is Jamaica's soul music. It evolved from many influences, all pulled together and fused into its distinctive beat and rebel lyrics. It is flamboyant, a tropical rock and roll with echoes of African drums, and emphasis on the second and fourth beats. But the music Bob Marley loved and made his own had to struggle hard to be accepted. "Monotonous, boring idiot music," it was called. "Dull stupid West Indian music", even "illiterate black music" or "garden-boy music".

These comments and attitudes came not only from the white Jamaicans, but from many black Jamaicans, and also the outside world. European and American DJs wouldn't play reggae on their shows. If DJs wouldn't give reggae a chance, there was little hope of it reaching their millions of listeners.

The people's music

Digging right back to the roots of reggae, it becomes clear why the music is so strongly associated with struggle and endurance. The roots lie in the days of slavery, when slave musicians imitated the music of their masters. Quadrille, or Katreel as it was known in Jamaica, resembled Scottish reels, polkas, and the English quadrilles. Cedella Booker's uncle played a four-string banjo in a Quadrille group. He would have been accompanied by a couple of guitars, a fife, and maybe a fiddle. The first music Bob Marley ever heard was his great uncle's band playing round dances like "Titanic", or "Jane and Louisa".

And yet, mingled with this European sound were the heartbeat drums of Africa, the heavy insistent beat that originated on the distant continent where slaves were

"Reggae means comin' from the people, y'know? Like a everyday thing. Like from the ghetto. From majority. Everyday thing that people use like food, we just put music to it and make a dance out of it. Reggae mean regular people who are suffering, and don't have what they want."

Toots Hibbert, from "Reggae Bloodlines".

17

sold and exported to the Spanish settlers in the Caribbean. This African influence, along with a Spanish sound, gave birth to a music that rural Jamaicans hailed as their own, "the people's music". This was called "Mento", and it flourished at the brams, or country dances, in the 1920s and 1930s. The spirit of Mento lived on and became a vital feature of reggae. The oppressed had found a voice.

The Wailing Wailers

"Reggae music is one of the greatest, one of the greatest musics you know," Bob Marley once said, "cause you dance the whole night and it keeps you in a mood...You love yourself when you dance reggae music. You proud of yourself, that you come like you're born again. Music can carry you to heaven...carry you all about to some place you don't know...why reggae music so nice is because it's a proud music."

But back in 1964, playing in the kitchen of his friend W. Vincent "Tartar" Ford, Bob could hardly have imagined the fame and success that would be his. He was still welding, still shifting round from friend to relative. Nevertheless, with the flair for leadership he was beginning to show, he tried to bring some organization to the music that he and his friends - Tosh, Bunny, and Junior Braithwaite - were so obsessed by. He formed the "reggae college". Then, when two girls turned up to provide backing vocals, the Wailing Wailers were born.

Bob was always the driving force in the group. He had a commanding presence that marked him out as a natural leader, yet he was calm and good-natured too.

"Anyone who cry out for righteousness and justice is a wailer," Marley once said. Kingston, in the early 1960s was a very apt place to be wailing. The living was hard for the slum families of Kingston 12. The Wailing Wailers had the support of some good people in the Jamaican music scene - people like Joe Higgs, who nurtured in Bob an appreciation of jazz, and Clement "Sir Coxsone" Dodd, in whose Studio One the band recorded their first singles. "I'm Still Waiting" and "It Hurts To Be Alone" spent months on the Jamaican charts and even made minor hits in Europe - but the

By the time Bob Marley and the Wailers became known internationally, in the early 1970s, they had given up the smooth-tailored, short-haired look (below). Fans in 1975 would have seen them with the wild, long dreadlocks that were a sign of their Rastafarian beliefs. At the height of his fame, Bob usually wore the same old denim shirts on stage. He was buried in one of his denim jackets.

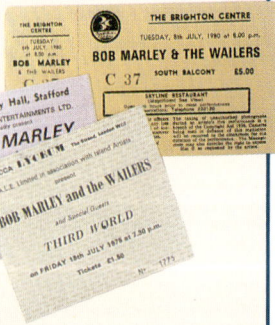

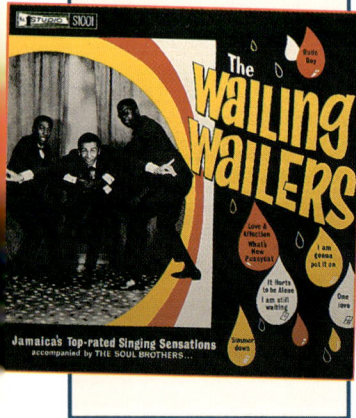

Wailers were still waiting for any financial reward to their efforts. Coxsone was not about to make their fortunes for them.

However, his contribution to Bob's musical education was worth more than money could buy. By introducing him to jazz, and American Rhythm and Blues with its shuffle rhythm and split beat, Coxsone ensured that reggae would take on board yet another

The Wailers (top left to right): Al Anderson, Alvin "Seeco" Paterson, Bob Marley, Carlton Barrett. (Bottom left to right): Junior Marvin, Aston "Family Man" Barrett, Tyrone Downie, and Earl "Wire" Lindo.

major influence. Bob and the other Wailing Wailers started listening to early rhythm and blues bands, like The Drifters and The Moonglows.

Rhythm and blues originated in Memphis, Tennessee, and it resembled the Jamaican Mento. Jamaican rhythm and blues imitated that of New Orleans. The similarities are not surprising: the American radio station, WINZ, could be picked up clearly in the West Indies and farm workers going to and fro from the islands to the mainland brought back wonderful stories about the Americans' casual manners and their expansive lifestyle.

The "systems" men

While the Wailing Wailers were absorbing jazz, the men in the music studios of West Kingston were playing their part in opening Jamaica to the new reggae music. Although equipment was scarce and money tight, mobile DJs, called "systems" men, packed their sound systems into rickety vans and toured the island, bringing reggae, the people's music, to the people. They hired out halls, and spent hours assembling their equipment, and then hours packing it all away again to head on to the next village.

If earnings from the singles weren't exactly lining the Wailers' pockets, at least they were blaring out from the speakers of the systems men right across Jamaica. This was "grass roots" reggae, music in the early stages of its development, still trying out new sounds, new beats, picking up new influences. The words had "dread" quality - they dealt with the living conditions, the political situation, with hardship and Rude Boy rage, with the things that really mattered to the people who were listening. "One good thing about music," sang the Wailing Wailers, "when it hits you, you feel no pain" ("Trench Town Rock"). And "No chains around my feet but I'm not free – I know I am bound here in captivity" ("Concrete Jungle").

Bongo

One of the main music talents of this time who influenced Bob Marley was the famous trombonist, Don Drummond. In his music, he wrote lyrically about hardship, but he was also tormented by the Rude Boy's helpless rage against the world he found himself in.

As well as being an important musician, Drummond helped promote black consciousness in the late 1960s, calling on blacks everywhere to be proud of their race and identity. The pain and suffering of his music came from the knowledge that blacks were meant to feel inferior. At the time, the term "bongo" was often heard in the West Indies. It described a type of music that was heavily influenced by African rhythms and instruments, but it also came from the word *Bungu* - a Nigerian Hausa word meaning ugly, illiterate, stupid.

"Reggae is created by people who have known suffering, who are disenfranchised, torn from their past and yet whose music is constantly redeemed by hope."

Roger Steffens,
from "L.A. Weekly", 1979.

In the spirit

There was another important aspect of Drummond's life that influenced Bob: Drummond belonged to the Rastafarian religion. Now in his late teens, Bob was being increasingly drawn to the Rastafari.

His music had already been deeply rooted in religion, beginning with the gospel songs his mother sang. Gospel music lent an important feature to reggae: the "antiphony". This is when a preacher (or lead singer) sings a few bars, establishing the rhythm, and these are then answered in harmony by the congregation (or backing vocalists). The idea behind this kind of call-and-response is that leader and congregation are drawn close by the rhythmic call and the fervent response. This point of contact is the starting point from which they go on to sing together as a single body, sharing what they feel and believe.

Reggae and Rastafari are entwined together in the music. The Rasta rhythm is a two-beat riff with beats from three membrane drums, made from barrels with goatskin stretched over the top. The largest drum is the repeater, which holds the melody in a trance-like rhythm. The other two drums are smaller and higher pitched. For Rastas, reggae exists not only to give pleasure to both player and listener, but to give praise to Jah, a shortened version of Jehovah, the Rasta word for God. The word "reggae" literally means "to the king" in Latin.

Marcus Garvey in 1922: his vision was of an independent black state in Africa, where blacks would no longer be in a minority. He founded the Universal Negro Improvement Association (UNIA) and swept through America preaching its doctrine of worldwide unity among Negroes.

A suffering people

Slowly, the teachings of Marcus Garvey, said by some to be the founder of the Rastafari religion, began to mean something to Marley. "We are the descendants of a suffering people," said Garvey, "we are the descendants of people determined to suffer no longer." The Rastafari religion embraced not only Bob Marley's faith, but his musical tastes and his politics - the fight for freedom for black people all over the world.

Many people who came in contact with Bob described his calmness, his sensitivity, and the feeling he generated that he was at peace with himself. Bob attributed this peace to the inspiration of his god.

Above: The Caribbean islands and Africa with Jamaica and Angola highlighted. The black slave population of Jamaica was largely imported from Africa in the sixteenth century. Marley's Rastafari message was based on the "back to Africa" theme of Marcus Garvey's teachings. The black people would rule their own country free from white rulers.

Opposite: Rastafarians use music as a means of expressing their beliefs and praising Jah, their god. They quote from the King James Bible – Bob took his own weathered copy with him when he went on tour.

"To me, the word love is God," he said. "That is my meaning of love...God himself is love." But this is a typically vague description of the beliefs that motivated him from his late teens. The story behind Rastafari is a rich, sometimes confusing, tale. There is contention about how the religion was actually started, whether by Marcus Garvey, or with the "Holy Piby", or "Black Man's Bible", which was published in 1924.

Why should I lose hope?

Whether Garvey founded Rastafari or not, he was certainly a very influential figure in the life of Bob Marley. He was one of those people who sees injustice and is determined to resist it. He was born on August 17, 1887, in Marley's home parish of St. Ann. He journeyed through the West Indies in the early years of the century, and all around him he saw the same conditions: the white people reigned, the black people served.

He went further afield - to South America, to Europe. Everywhere it was the same. "Where is the black man's

government?" he asked. "Where is his king and kingdom?" The more oppression and discrimination he saw, the more determined he became. "Why should I lose hope," he demanded, "and take a back place in this age of progress?"

Like Martin Luther King after him, and other black civil rights leaders, Garvey sought an identity for blacks; and his search for this identity inevitably brought him, in 1913, to Africa. Ethiopia had long been considered, by Africans and blacks everywhere, to be the cradle of civilization. At a time when only two African nations were independent, Marcus Garvey stood up and claimed Africa as the home of all blacks, wherever they were. He began trying to instil a sense of pride and purpose in a people so used to slavery and serving, they had almost forgotten what freedom meant.

As their motto, he chose "One God, One Aim, One Destiny". This linked belief, a sense of identity and the wish for unification with their ideal of a return to Africa. Black people must no longer cower before their white rulers, Garvey said. And he wanted the change to take place peacefully. He saw the destiny of black people as a return to the proud, self-respecting race they had been in Africa: and to accompany this spiritual return, he had a grand vision of a physical return journey. He set up a shipping line called The Black Star, and bought land in Liberia, in West Africa. These were to be the foundations for a grand-scale repatriation of Africans - the black people were going home.

But Garvey's dream came to nothing. His "Back To Africa" movement collapsed. In 1922, the American government charged him with fraud, and he was deported. At first, he was scorned even in his native Jamaica. But he was credited with a prophecy, supposedly given in one of his speeches to Jamaica's poorest blacks, that a "Black King" would be born in Africa.

A black king crowned

On November 2, 1930, it seemed to those who believed in the prophecy that it had come true. A man called Ras Tafari was crowned Emperor of Ethiopia. He took the name Haile Selassie, which means "Power of the Trinity." "Ras" is a title given to all Ethiopian royalty.

The people who believed Garvey's proclamation, long waiting for their Black King, were convinced that he had been crowned at last.

However, more recent research claims that Garvey never presented himself as a prophet, that in fact he was very critical of Haile Selassie. And it is suggested that the true origins of Rastafari are found in the Holy Piby.

The Holy Piby was viewed as the closest thing to their first bible. It was written in the ancient Ethiopian language of Amharic, which was believed to be the first language of mankind. No one knows for sure where it originated, whether it was found by Reverend Charles Goodridge in Panama, or compiled by Robert Althyi Rogers during the years 1913-17. However it was discovered, and by 1925 it was being printed in New Jersey and shipped to South Africa. That year, Goodridge brought its message to Jamaica.

The organized churches in Jamaica opposed this heretical bible, and Goodridge fled with his followers to the bush land of East Jamaica. Here, the Piby brotherhood grew, insisting that one day the order would be reversed and the reviled black race would, once again, become Jah's chosen people. The early popes had

Emperor Haile Selassie of Ethiopia. Originally Ras Tafari Makonnen, the grandson of King Selassie Shoa, he was crowned Emperor in 1930 and claimed to be the 225th ruler in a direct line descended from Solomon and Sheba. Rastas believe he was the Messiah, or living God.

Above: The African influence on Rastafarians is seen in the long matted dreadlocks, which are also worn by the Masai warriors of Kenya.

Left: An African shrine figure. When Marcus Garvey told Jamaicans, "We are the descendants of a people determined to suffer no more," he meant Africans.

distorted the true bible, they said, making God white.

Garvey had nothing to do with the Piby movement, but when he tried to return to Jamaica, the middle-class paper there, the *Daily Gleaner,* associated him with the bush rebels in order to discredit him. He made brave attempts to deny any connection, but his reputation among religious blacks was ruined. Faced with open hostility, he went to England in 1935 and died there five years later.

However, throughout the 1920s, some Jamaicans had begun to respond to his message, and to see the importance of his call to unite under one God.

Bob gave me strength

By 1934, there was a solid following of Rastafari in Kingston. By 1965, Jamaicans were so enthusiastic about his ideas that they bestowed on Garvey one of the highest titles of respect of their country: Marcus Garvey became a national hero of Jamaica.

Bob Marley was profoundly affected by the teachings of Garvey. Some people felt daunted by the religion that surrounded him and filled Marley's music. His own mother, Cedella, felt something of this, too, when her son first told her he had "sighted" Rastafari. This was when he visited her in America when he was eighteen. "I used to pray and ask the Lord to change him," she said later. "Because I said I am not a Rasta and I don't have anyone in the family who is a Rasta...I always talk to God about it." Then she laughed. "But then at the time I was thinking God [was] white."

That night in 1963, Bob told his mother that she, too, was a Rasta, and always had been. He told her she was on the right track - because she had faith, and now he wanted to tell her that God, whom he called Jah (from the Jehovah of the Bible), was none other than His Imperial Majesty, the Emperor Haile Selassie of Ethiopia. It was a hard message for a woman who for thirty-five years had followed the Christian faith. But Cedella listened to her son as he sat with her that night, quoting scripture and reasoning.

They talked together from 9 p.m. till 3 a.m. "Bob give me a lot of strength," she reflected years later. "Especially that morning...when he blessed me before he

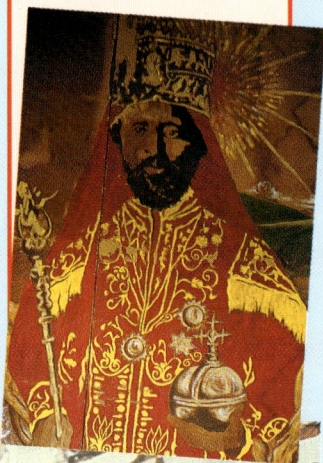

Below: Haile Selassie visited Jamaica in April 1966. His visit elevated Rastafari almost to the level of a national religion in Jamaica. Bottom: Bob looked to Africa for his real roots and was passionate about seeing Africans free to govern their own countries.

departed. I used to feel bad," she concluded simply, "but now I'm feeling perfect."

Bob was a complex person: in his music and his public life, he seemed to display many different sides to his character. Sometimes he was rebellious, sometimes gentle, sometimes humorous. But one thing that most people who spoke to him seemed to feel was a strength, the same strength his mother spoke of.

Bob Marley as a live performer was an event. His inspiration and power, his dynamism and charisma, made his presence on stage electric.

His performances were sometimes lifted out of the ordinary. "In concert he gets very emotionally involved," his wife, Rita, later revealed. "He closes his eyes, that mean he lock off this world completely, on a different level of communicating. It is a natural spiritual thing that happens to him each time he goes on stage. He gets involved spiritually. He gets in spirit."

Marley's biographers, Whitney and Hussey, said, "He translated into music, in a remarkable style, the aspirations, pain and feeling of millions of people throughout the world."

Rastafari

"It's not politic[s], it's really talkin' about roots," Bob told an interviewer who asked what Rastafari is all about. "And Exodus is really Exodus from Babylon to freedom. Seen?" "Seen" is the Rasta way of saying "Understand?" and it's an example of how the Rastas tailor the English language so that it is distinctively theirs. Exodus, the name of both a song and an album of Marley's, means the departure of the Israelites from Egypt, led by Moses. In the song "Exodus", Marley relates this original exodus to the return of Rasta to Ethiopia:

"The Rastafari religion has given the Jamaican people a pride they never previously felt. It has given them a direction and a sense of communal purpose. It is taking them out of their immediate misery, giving them the strength to build up and move away from their ghetto past."

Bob Marley.

> *"We're the generation*
> *Who trod through great tribulation...*
> *Jah come to...wipe away transgression*
> *And set the captives free.*
> *Exodus, movement of Jah people."*
>
> *"Exodus"*

Babylon, on the other hand, stands for any evil force - whether a place, a person, or a culture.

Rastas say they make the language more positive. "You can't be two things at one time," explained Bob. "If you positive, you have to be positive. If you negative, you have to be negative. Want to cut the negative thing out entirely." Marley wasn't only telling black people to unite and stand tall with pride, he wanted his music to reach all people, especially the oppressed - the "downpressed" as he called them.

A way of life

When anyone calls Rastafari "Rastafarianism", it grates harshly on Rasta ears. They reject the description of their whole way of life as just another "ism". The word is RASTA-FAR-I: Rasta signifies permanence, a state of mind, a way of life, a peace.

Rasta life is dictated by strict codes. Their diet does not include any food that is not "ital", or pure. For example, alcohol, dairy products, breads made with white flour, tobacco, meat, sugar-based drinks, and salt are all excluded. Rastas do not cut their hair and as it grows they shape it into long, matted lengths or "dreadlocks". They take this directive from the Bible, the book of Leviticus, chapter 21, verse 5: "They shall not make baldness upon their head, neither shall they shave off the corner of their beard, nor make any cuttings in their flesh."

Rasta women take a very servile role in the Rastafari way of life. Their main functions are as child-bearers, fire-builders and cooks. They are not allowed to wear any make-up or perfume or to dress outrageously. They are considered unclean when menstruating and cannot join in any discussions of importance. Nor can women smoke from the "chillum", the clay pipe from which Rastas smoke marijuana or herb.

The smoking of herb, also called "ganja", plays a central role in the life of Rastas. They believe it helps them to think and to meditate better, they feel it gives them a common understanding so that they can unite with their brothers and sisters. Rastas claim that the profound experiences sometimes brought on by smoking ganja increases their sensitivity - both

In the Rastafari way of life, women are not given many rights. From the age of twelve, girls are expected to work with their mothers looking after the large families. Most would hope to be pregnant before they were eighteen and if they weren't, would be worried that they were not attractive. Their lives would then revolve around bringing up a family.

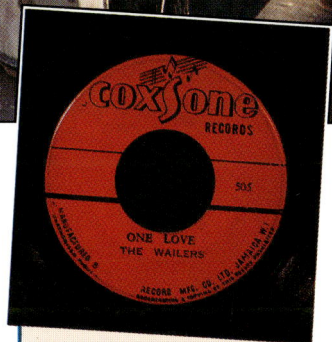

physically and mentally. And they believe it is good because it is natural and comes from the earth.

Bob, although he never touched alcohol, believed in the goodness of herb: "When you smoke herb, herb reveal itself to you. All the wickedness you do, the herb reveal it to yourself, your conscience, show yourself up clear, because herb make you meditate. Is only a natural ting and it grow like a tree."

To America ...

In 1965, the same year that Marcus Garvey was given the title of Jamaican national hero, Bob and the Wailing Wailers were making singles for Clement "Sir Coxsone" Dodd. In this year too, Bob met his future wife, Rita Anderson. Rita used to watch the Wailers pass her home on their way to Coxsone's studio. She'd chat to them, and try to persuade them to listen to her sing. When they did, she impressed them so much that

Top: One of the mobile sound systems, bringing music to people much too poor to buy records. Above: Clement "Sir Coxsone" Dodd recorded Bob Marley's earliest songs. Opposite: Bob's dreadlocks meant total freedom to him; he wore them "as a crown".

she was taken on as the lead singer of a band called The Soulettes. Later, she sang with the Wailers, too. In the meantime, Bob found himself taking more than a professional interest in sunny Rita.

Then, in 1966, Braithwaite left the band, and Bob thought he'd try his luck in Delaware, where his mother was. He and Rita were married, and he set out for America the next day. He was twenty-one years old. "He's a people's person," was how Rita described her husband. "There is no night for him, no rest. There was always people around, just to be with Bob." The couple would have four children: Cedella, David (Ziggy), Stephen and Stephanie. They also brought up Rita's daughter from a previous relationship, Sharon. Bob had many extra-marital affairs, and had seven other children by different women - although some wilder stories put the number of his offspring at over twenty. For Rita, this was painful to know. "Of course it bothered me," she said years later. "It would have bothered anyone...[but] what Bob and I had was something special that God ordained. Ours was more than a husband-and-wife relationship, it was as if we had to do something for our people, to become a symbol for our time."

... and back

For a year, Bob Marley worked at odd jobs to support his young wife, sometimes using the welding skills picked up so reluctantly back in Kingston. But in 1967, he received a draft card: the American government wanted him to fight in the Vietnam War. Violence went against Bob's nature, so he returned to Rita in Jamaica, where he joined up again with Bunny and Tosh.

In the year he was away, the two had been playing as much as ever. Coxsone, however, was paying as little as ever, so although Bob released a few more singles with him - including one called "This Man Is Back" - he decided instead to open a record store with Bunny and Tosh. The store, on Beeston Street, was managed by Allan "Skill" Cole, who was to prove a great friend to Bob. It was tough, trying to keep the store and the band going at the same time, but The Wailing Wailers managed to release hit singles, such as "Stir it up" and "Nice Time" on their own label, "Wailin' Soul".

Rhythmic rot

While the three were struggling to keep the record store going, reggae music was still struggling to find acceptance in the international music market.

In spite of the success of Desmond Dekker and the Aces' song "The Israelites" in 1960, there were deep prejudices among rock music fans against reggae. It just wasn't taken seriously. It was a rough sound. It lowered the standards of music, they thought. The owner of Island Records, Chris Blackwell, described the situation as he saw it: "Reggae up until the Wailers' first album was perceived as rather quirky music in general...It wasn't a music that had any respect."

Blackwell became a key figure in the future of reggae, and of Marley himself. In 1959, he had established Island Records in Jamaica, and three years later he had taken the label to London. Island had released a lot of reggae and ska (a kind of big band music that grew out of rhythm & blues) in the early and mid sixties. Millie Small got to No. 2 in Britain in 1964 with "My Boy Lollipop", on the Island label. She was really the first West Indian singer to make that kind of impact in the West. But Blackwell found the rock market so firmly set against the "rhythmic rot", as they perceived reggae, that he began to phase out reggae to rock bands, like Jethro Tull. He took no interest in the Wailing Wailers in these early years of their career.

While Chris Blackwell was temporarily giving up on reggae, another label was established in 1968 that would greatly help to publicize the music. This was Trojan records, set up to try and finally overcome the prejudices against reggae. In Britain, Radio One, took to playing Trojan music - "The Israelites" was released on this label. But for Bob Marley, aged twenty-three, lacking the support of any major label, this was still a precarious time.

If at first you don't succeed...

1968 was a tough year. The Wailing Wailers were not being paid for their hit singles, the record shop failed, and Bunny was put in prison for a year for possession of marijuana. Still penniless, Bob and Rita returned to St.

Ann for a while to try farming. This didn't work and Bob was made an offer by three Americans: the singer Johnny Nash, his manager, Danny Simms, and the arranger, Arthur Jenkins. These three formed the JAD label, and they wanted to sign Marley and the group to the label. Nash even paid for Bob to go to Europe to make an album and film score but, although the band did do backing vocals on one album for JAD, the trip to Europe was a failure.

Bob returned ready to team up with Tosh and Bunny, now released from prison, to try again. This time, they shortened their name from The Wailing Wailers to The Wailers. They were taken on by the Upsetter label, and here, at last, in 1968-9, they began to make it.

Upsetter was owned by Lee Perry, an innovator in sound production who helped to incorporate new rhythms and eccentric African-sounding percussion into reggae. It was Perry who told The Wailers to make their songs sound like real reggae with a heavy thudding beat. He also advised Bob to concentrate on his vocals which tended to be "lazy". The collaboration between Lee Perry and The Wailers was a tremendous success. Bob was later to call Perry "a genius".

"Smash the world!"

The early months of the 1970s still brought a series of ups and downs to The Wailers. They were tired of working for exacting studio producers, and being paid miserably into the bargain. They decided to strike out on their own, leaving the Upsetter label and forming one on their own.

The new label was christened "Tuff Gong", after Marley's nickname from the ghetto, and because life in the music business really was "tough going".

The new label, and the addition of two more musicians - brothers Carlton and Aston Barrett - proved just the stroke of fortune they needed. "The Wailers was the best vocal group," said Aston later, "and [our] group was the best little backing band at the time, so we say why don't we just come together and smash the world!" The hit singles began to come thick and fast: "Root Rock Reggae", "Smile Jamaica" and "One Drop".

"Why do you look so sad and forsaken," they sang in

Tuff Gong records was the label Bob had wanted so much to start up himself. He wrote "Trench Town Rock" during his time farming in St. Ann in 1967, but it wasn't released until 1970. Early Tuff Gong labels had a space left blank for the song title to be filled in by hand.

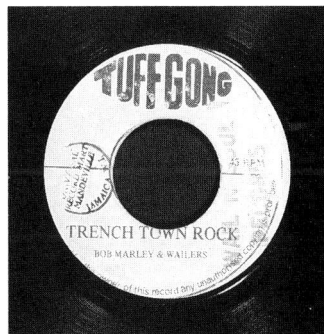

"Coming In From The Cold". "When one door is closed, don't you know another is open."

Doors were certainly opening for The Wailers now. Carlton Barrett was considered to be Jamaica's best bass player, and his brother Aston, "Family Man", was widely believed to be the best drummer. With their talents they brought huge enthusiasm and a touch of Rude Boy dread to The Wailers.

Marley's contract with Island Records, the most important independent record company in the world, lasted almost a full decade – ending with the "Uprising" album, that was released in May 1980.

Signed with Island

While The Wailers were warming up to conquer the world, reggae itself was finally bursting through the international barriers of prejudice and suspicion. At Island Records, Chris Blackwell was changing his mind about it. In his opinion, rock music was becoming stale.

When he heard Marley and The Wailers' singles that were creating such a stir in the Caribbean, he took a decision that was to shape the future of the band, and of reggae itself. Paying a staggering eight-thousand-pound advance for their first album, Blackwell signed The Wailers with Island Records.

Something different

It was 1971. The Wailers were the first reggae alternative to rock to hit the international music scene. Most importantly, they opened up reggae to a massive audience it had never reached before: white youth.

Chris Blackwell had long been hoping to sign The Wailers to Island, and they were to prove a fantastic team. Before, the reggae market had always been geared to the release of singles. Reggae fans were poorer than rock fans, they couldn't afford to buy albums, and there was no tradition of grouping songs to form a unified album, as there was in rock music. Most rock fans were from the prosperous areas of the world - Europe and North America. They bought albums, and the record companies knew this, and recognized the profit to be made from investing in albums. Reggae albums, such as they were, consisted of collections of greatest hits.

Blackwell saw all this changing, and that's why he paid such a handsome advance for what was, in effect, the first reggae album ever. Blackwell had an intense feeling for the music market and he could sense trends instinctively. He knew the reggae from the late sixties that rock fans hated, and he knew that Marley and the Wailers were something different, something fresh.

"Their dream lives on"

The magazine *Black Echoes* saw it in more dramatic and racial terms: "The white kids have lost their heroes," it announced in a June 1976 issue. "Jagger has become a wealthy socialite, Dylan a mellow home-loving man, even Lennon has little to say anymore. So along comes this guy with amazing screw-top hair, and he's singing about 'burning and looting' and 'brainwash education'...Their dream lives on."

If The Wailers were to become the stuff of the white kids' dreams, it was Chris Blackwell's money that made it possible. He offered superior recording equipment and high standards of sound. He judged correctly that if Jamaican music was to appeal to anyone outside Jamaica, it would need money pumped into it. Accordingly, The Wailers' first album, "Catch a Fire", while recorded in Jamaica, was mixed and dubbed by Blackwell in London. He cleaned up the quality of the recording, and gave the album a more "produced" sound that he knew rock fans had come to expect.

Catching fire

It worked. That is, it worked in the market Blackwell was aiming for. It really proved the first serious reggae challenge to rock, and it left rock fans ready for more. Marley and The Wailers went on tour. They played two concerts in 1973: with Marvin Gaye in Jamaica and later with Sly and the Family Stone in the United States.

But, curiously, the album was poorly received in Jamaica itself. The band didn't even want it released there until certain changes had been made to Blackwell's "produced" version. Ironically, they insisted that the original heavy bass rhythm be mixed in again. Blackwell had removed it, thinking it was too close to the old "roots" reggae for his audience. For the same reason, he speeded the whole album up by a beat, and added more guitars, and more keyboards. Blackwell knew his market.

But the real reggae fans, the Jamaicans themselves, distrusted the foreign instruments and musicians that featured on the album. Just as Marley finally got his big break, reaching fans all over the world, it seemed he was drifting further and further from his home community.

West Indians feel very strongly about their music, and it's contribution to making them a proud people again. "Uprooted from our motherland, Africa," explain two reggae fans, "we were stripped of our manhood, heritage, and culture, and denied permission to practise our religion or partake in anything musical that was part of our African culture." Marley was not afraid to cry out for justice for the oppressed people of Kingston in his songs. In the last one he wrote, "Redemption Song", he calls on the "downpressed" to:

> *"Emancipate your selves from mental slavery*
> *None but ourselves can free our minds*
> *Have no fear for atomic energy*
> *Cause none a them can stop the time*
> *How long shall they kill our prophets*
> *While we stand aside and look...*
> *Won't you help to sing, these song of freedom*
> *Cause all I ever had, redemption songs."*
> *"Redemption Song"*

"[Bob Marley]...a man who understands racism, who understands poverty, who understands all the hurts, and he didn't let it defeat him. He set out to share his joy, his love, his great respect, his religion, his spiritual power with the whole world."

Dick Gregory, a black social activist, introducing Bob Marley at the AMANDLA concert in the USA, 1979.

Fun-loving Bob

At this point, Bob Marley was twenty-eight, and had been married to Rita for seven years. His career was just taking off on a massive scale, and Rita was there to support him, singing backing vocals for The Wailers with the I-Threes. Even their children were musical - Bob later wrote a selection of songs for The Melody Makers, the group made up of the four eldest Marley children, Sharon, Cedella, Ziggy and Stephen.

Those who knew Bob closely described him as a gentle, fun-loving man who was happiest when children were around.

"Children were in the room when Bob was composing, and it was children who Bob was singing to," said one biographer, Stephen Davis.

"As the pressure of international fame and cultural

Overleaf: The Wailers' 1973 album "Burnin'" confronted the issues of the political wars heating up in the slums of Kingston. The people were under curfew, and the lyrics of the title track "Burnin' and Lootin'" express the hopelessness they felt: "Burnin' all illusions tonight." By early 1974, a state of emergency had been declared in Jamaica and there were tanks and troops in the capital, Kingston. "Jamaica ... really need a direction," Bob said in an interview.

power built up around him, Bob Marley was the most relaxed, the least shy and withdrawn, the most himself when kids were around."

Still raging

The Wailers on stage presented a vitally important message, with their dreadlocks and tams (hats) in the Rasta stripes: red for the bloodshed of the people, gold for wealth and green for the fertility of the earth.

Rastas had always looked highly distinctive, and The Wailers were holding on more and more firmly to their Rasta belief. They dressed to fit their way of life, just as they made the English language express their beliefs uniquely. They wore loose, comfortable clothes. Their long, uncombed dreadlocks, as well as being a sign of freedom, could be traced back to the African Masai warriors, who still wear dreadlocks in Africa.

But side by side with this peaceful calm image, Bob Marley still raged. Songs like "Get up, Stand up" were the kind of rebel sound that really sold Marley to the white youth.

"Get up, stand up
Stand up for your rights
Get up, stand up
Don't give up the fight
We're sick and tired of your easing kissing game
To die and go to Heaven in Jesus' name
We know and understand
Almighty God is a living man
You can fool some people sometimes
But you can't fool all the people
All the time
And now we've seen the light
We gonna stand up for our rights."

"Get Up, Stand Up"

The years 1972 to 1976 were a time of great change in youth culture. Marley's words were like a match to a pile of dry brushwood; disillusioned young people heard him talking directly to them. "I could relate strongly," said one fan, "even though I wasn't black...you know 'Stop pushing me Mr. Boss Man', loads of them songs...and the ones about freedom too. Cos I hated school, I felt I was captive by the school, and by people in authority."

And Robin Denselow of *The Guardian* wrote, "He was everything that rock in the sixties had strived for: a genuine street poet thrown up from a poor background, who articulated the passions, hopes and faith of the people around him, much as the great American blues singers had done".

It was possibly the song "No Woman, No Cry" that catapulted Bob Marley and The Wailers to the heart of the rock and pop stage. They performed this song live at the London Lyceum in 1974, on their second British tour.

"In this great future
You can't forget your past
So dry your tears I say."

"No Woman, No Cry"

By now, they were being introduced as a rock group - and yet they had lost none of their reggae traits. It seemed, at last, as if rock and reggae had forgotten their differences and embraced - as if fans in both camps had realized that it was the quality of the music that mattered, and not whether they were used to it or not. For young people everywhere, The Wailers were seen to be creating music for change, as well as producing an exciting and vibrant sound.

> *"Our music is there to deal with the conditions where we come from. The music is like the news. The music influence the people. The music do everything for the people; the music tell the people what to do in Jamaica."*
>
> Bob Marley.

Solo

Nevertheless, in spite of their success, Bob's oldest music mates decided they wanted to go on to something new. Peter Tosh and Bunny Livingston left The Wailers after "Burnin'". Both of them went on to have great solo careers of their own.

Some people felt that Island had quickly singled out Marley as the genius and key figure of the group and pushed Tosh and Bunny to one side in the process. But the way Tosh looked on it was this: "When I left the Wailers it was not directly any conflict between Bob and me...I was at that time decorating what was inside of Bob to make it beautiful, and the time had to come for me to decorate what was inside of me, so I did."

As a solo artist, Bob Marley brought out the "Natty Dread" album, though he had backing vocals from the I-Threes on it (Rita, Judy Mowatt, and Marcia Griffiths). He also had help from the Barrett brothers, Joe Higgs, and Al Anderson. "Natty Dread" really pushed Bob's "Rasta Rebel" image. Even the title of the album was an attempt to appeal to a wider audience. It was originally to be called "Knotty Dread", but Blackwell felt "knotty" should become "natty", which meant fashionable, hip, cool. Knotty was a bit militant: although Bob was pushing a rebel image at this time, it was rebellion through music and ideas, and not through violence.

Marley was essentially a very peaceful man, as he demonstrated many times throughout his life. "I and I not come to fight flesh and blood, But spiritual wickedness in high and low places," he sang in "So Much Things To Say". "Natty Dread" became the sound of reggae, and Bob Marley its greatest star.

Rolling Stone
Bob Marley
Rastaman with a Bullet
By Ed McCormack
THE BEACH BOYS TEST THE WATER
BY JIM MILLER
PAT MOYNIHAN
Ruling-Class Hero
By Timothy Crouse
JAMAICA AT WAR
Stalking the Beast of Babylon
By Michael Thomas
JIMMY PAGE
Beats the Devil
By Cameron Crowe

Rastaman

In his next album, "Rastaman Vibration", he set down all his firmest convictions. It was an album that displayed the different sides of this complex man. In "Crazy Baldheads" he was aggressive, a Rude Boy to the roots:

> "Didn't my people before me
> Slave for this country
> Now you look at me with scorn."
>> "Crazy Baldheads"

And he voiced his disgust over human greed:

> "Don't forget your history
> Know your destiny
> In the abundance of water
> The fool is thirsty
> Rat race, rat race, rat race
> Oh it's a disgrace to see the
> Human race in a rat race, rat race".
>> "Rat Race"

Then, in "Johnny Was", he sang mournfully, and in "Who The Cap Fit", he lamented "Man to man is so unjust, You just don't know who to trust." But he could always laugh, and laugh he did, singing "We're bubbling on the Top 100" in "Roots Rock reggae", which bubbled not only on the top one hundred but made the US top ten. "Rastaman Vibration" received a staggering six hundred thousand advance orders.

After the 1975 tours, in which Bob played to all races and won over millions of disillusioned rock fans, he was firmly established at the pinnacle of stardom.

This was a very steady point in his career. In the uncertain early days he had been a Rude Boy and a soul rebel. He had challenged authority - and although these aspects of his character never changed, as Rastaman he seemed to combine them happily, so that rebel existed alongside peace-loving Rasta.

Smile Jamaica

Precisely as Marley was achieving a unity in his music and his image, Jamaica was being torn apart. In the run-up to the 1976 elections, tempers on the island were

Opposite: Marley made the cover of "Rolling Stone" when he was shot – a victim of his country's political violence, although in a "New York Times" interview, he later suggested he might have been shot because of jealousy.

Below: Bob was a keen footballer. There was nearly always a game of soccer going on in the yard of 56 Hope Road.

running very high. On one side, there was the prime minister, Michael Manley, and his People's National Party. On the other stood Edward Seaga and the Jamaican Labour Party. Neither side would give an inch in the battle for leadership, and the Jamaicans themselves fell into two sharply divided groups.

To Bob Marley, politics was just another "ism". The clashes that were taking place in the streets of Kingston seemed like the words of his songs come true: "It takes a revolution / To make a solution." A hungry mob is an angry mob, he had always warned, and now the poor of Trenchtown and the Concrete Jungle were rising up against years of poverty and suffering.

Things got so bad that the Prime Minister imposed a state of emergency. "Heavy Manners" (Jamaican censorship) was imposed, in an effort to cool the atmosphere. Even Marley's music came under the ban: songs such as "Rat Race", "Crazy Baldheads" and "Who The Cap Fit" were outlawed.

But instead of revolution, Marley believed this was a time for peace. He watched his country writhe in the grip of political fever, and he felt moved to give something to his people in return for all they had given him. To this end, he planned a "Smile Jamaica" concert, a mark of gratitude to the nation.

A killer strikes

Then came the assassination attempt. On the afternoon before the concert, Bob, Rita, Don Taylor and others were rehearsing in the house at 56 Hope Road, when five gunmen burst in and sprayed them with bullets. All three were hit, but only Taylor - who dived in front of Bob - was seriously hurt. It seemed that political fever burned so high among the militants of the Jamaican Labour Party that they tried to kill a man who was trying to improve the situation.

Bob felt able and determined to go ahead with the concert even though he was unable to play his guitar with his wounded arm. And he did. He sang one song, "War", before an ecstatic crowd and even displayed the wound on his arm, grinning, to the roars of the audience. "When I decided to play this concert there were no

May 12, 1976: Bob waits outside the x-ray department of Kingston's University Hospital. The assassin's bullet grazed his breastbone and left arm. Rita was wounded by a piece of bullet that lodged between her scalp and skull; Bob's manager, Don Taylor, came off worst, hit by five bullets. Nevertheless, Bob went ahead with the "Smile Jamaica" concert.

politics," he told them. "I wanted to play for the love of the people."

But Marley was shaken by the incident and it prompted a year abroad with his family. He needed time to slow down, and to come to terms with the blow dealt him just when he had everything to give. That year was later described as a time of exile, but he reasoned out his flight from Jamaica in the song "Running Away":

> *"I've got to protect my life*
> *And I don't want to live with no strife*
> *It is better to live on the house top*
> *Than to live in a house full of confusion*
> *So I made my decision and I left you."*
> *"Running Away"*

"De higher people in Jamaican government should clean up de dumps an' slums an' feed my people, my childran! Me read da paper an' me ashamed. Dat's why me must leave dis place an' return ta Africa. If Jamaica was me home, den me love Jamaica, and me wouldn't feel like me feel: dat dis place is not me home!"

Bob Marley.

Above: Bob with Stephen, his second son by Rita. Bob had a large number of children by different women and claimed he could recognize any child of his by their mouth.
Right: Bob with the I-Threes (Rita, Judy Mowatt and Marcia Griffiths) in 1977. By this time, he considered the backing singers as permanent members of the Wailers.

The album that emerged from this period of his life was his best-selling album ever: "Exodus". Blackwell introduced Junior Marvin to Marley around this time, and in 1977, Junior became the lead guitarist with Bob Marley and the Wailers.

"Exodus" spent a staggering fifty-six weeks on the British charts. It dealt honestly with Marley's response to the attempt on his life, and also introduced him singing love songs: one of the many sides of the man that came through in his music.

They keep us hungry

It wasn't this side of Marley, however, that disillusioned young rock fans were clinging to. Their hopes lay in the songs of rebellion and dread, they loved Marley when he sang to shock. The songs that they were most enthusiastic about were the ones that dealt with poverty and suffering and protest.

Around this time, rock was going stale, just as Blackwell had predicted. The themes were tame, and the danger somehow missing. The young people found it tough making sense of their world, as their music heroes became rich and complacent and stopped singing about the things that mattered.

For thousands of young whites in Europe and America, Bob Marley was singing about exactly these things so close to their hearts. "Political violence fill ya city...Don't involve Rasta...Rasta don't work for no CIA" ("Rat Race"). "Through political strategy/ They keep us hungry/And when you gonna get some food/Your brother got to be your enemy" ("Ambush"). They listened to these songs and felt that at last, someone was expressing exactly what they felt.

In 1976, a new and radical movement that worked on the desire to shock had sprung into being in Britain. It was called Punk.

Bob Marley felt he understood what was at the heart of punk: "A punk feel that English society do them no good," he said. "They want them roots." Whatever they wanted, they seemed to find it in reggae. Johnny Rotten of the Sex Pistols raved about reggae. The Clash recorded the Junior Marvin hit "Police and Thieves".

"He [Bob Marley] was, above all else, a symbol of hope and optimism for millions of fellow humans around the world."

From, "New Musical Express".

49

On-stage at the "One Love" Concert, April 22, 1978. The concert was planned to coincide with a truce between the Jamaican Labour and National People's Parties, and a cease-fire to the violence in the ghettos. To seal the truce, Marley was invited back to Jamaica, and his safety guaranteed from the killers who had caused his two-year exile.

"His [Marley's] fans come for the music, but it's the message they take away."

Jon Bradshaw, from the "Los Angeles Times", 1977.

And in return, Marley released "Punky Reggae Party", his own tribute to punk.

The second album Marley released from "exile" was "Kaya". This album was a further expression of the quiet side of Bob Marley, and it displeased some of his fans, who felt he had "gone soft". But he stood firm: at this point he knew exactly what he wanted to say in his music and he was going to say it. It is a measure of his maturity as a musician that he felt, "There comes a time when the artist can't follow the crowd. You have to be you and make the crowd follow you."

Politically, Bob felt he had moved on. "How long must I protest the same thing? I sing 'Get Up Stand Up' and up till now people don't get up. So must I still sing 'Get Up Stand Up'? I am not going to sing the same song again...I do not want to be a prisoner. I don't want to see people suffer and sing as if I'm glad to see people suffer and to make money off of that. I want people to live big and have enough."

It was just after "Kaya" was released that Bob received Claude Massop's invitation to return to Jamaica

50

for the "One Love One Peace" concert.

The peace treaty that Massop and Marshall had put together was designed to put an end, once and for all, to the political turmoil still troubling the island. Western Kingston had become a war-zone, with rival gangs roaming the streets and frequent shootings. Marley was not the only music man who had been gunned down: DJ General Echo was shot dead while loading speakers into his van.

So the treaty came as a ray of hope, and the concert on that April night in 1978 became one of the greatest musical events in the country's history. Marley and The Wailers were joined on-stage by Peter Tosh, Dennis Brown, Big Youth, and Jacob "Killer" Miller. The mood was one of jubilation - and then Marley made that famous gesture of reconciliation: joining the hands of Prime Minister Michael Manley and leader of the opposition, Edward Seaga, above his head. It was a wonderful day for Bob Marley.

There is work to be done

Even greater things were in store, however. It was also in 1978 that Marley made his first visit to Africa. This meant the world to him. He was returning, at last, to his roots, to Ethiopia.

Out of all he saw and heard in Africa grew the album "Survival" a year later. This was an album of revolutionary cries for justice and the righting of wrongs. "Africa Unite" was the message - "it's later than you think". His voice was full of rage for white people all over the world. "How can you be sitting there / Telling me that you care / When every time I look around / The people in suffering everywhere."

Back in his homeland, the carnage was continuing. In the run-up to the 1980 elections, more than eight hundred people were killed.

"We'll have to fight...Fight for our rights" Marley sang in the song "Zimbabwe". He had a special message for the African state that was at this time fighting fiercely for independence. Previously called Southern Rhodesia, it had been under British rule now for nearly a century, and the people wanted their freedom.

In their struggle, they adopted the song on "Survival"

Above: A member of the Jamaican drug mafia. On Marley's return to his homeland in March 1978, he made a tour through Kingston's worst ghettos as a demonstration of solidarity with the new peace movement. Nevertheless, the house on Hope Road was guarded by armed police.

as their anthem. For the soldiers living and fighting in the bush, Marley's words were their hope of success. For the women freedom fighters, "No Woman, No Cry" became their anthem.

Viva Zimbabwe!

Robert Mugabe, who became prime minister of Zimbabwe (formerly Rhodesia) when it gained independence in 1980. Bob Marley avidly supported Zimbabwe's struggle for freedom and his song "Zimbabwe" was adopted by Mugabe's followers in the bush as their anthem.

Finally, the struggle ended, and the Zimbabweans won the independence they had fought for. Under their new leader, Robert Mugabe, they prepared for the celebrations on April 18, 1980. First, the freedom fighters came out of the bush and once again walked free on the streets of their towns. For many, it was the first time in a long time that they had been able to "Get Up and Stand Up", without ducking bullets and running.

A personal invitation from Prime Minister Mugabe to share in Zimbabwe's independence celebrations was a great privilege for Bob Marley. He was the only foreign performer at the celebrations. The scenes of welcome at the airport were ecstatic.

The celebrations began. The repression of white rule was over; the Union Jack was lowered and the brilliant red, yellow, green and black flag of Zimbabwe raised. On-stage, Marley shared in the exultation of Zimbabwe, body and soul. As one American radio representative in Zimbabwe that day described it: "I think being in Zimbabwe at that time was personally for Bob, the highest point. I mean, no honorable mention or order of merit, no other moment could have been as significant."

Marley, the performer

The Viva Zimbabwe concert was the climax of his career. On stage, he was more full of life and spirit than ever. Reports of Bob performing live describe him becoming so caught up with the music, the beat, and his belief in what he was singing, that he sometimes seemed to go into a trance.

The same thing happened at the concert in Zimbabwe. There was trouble because the freedom fighters who had been fighting in the bush for independence, were not invited to the independence celebrations. When they heard the music, they came anyway, and

there were clashes with the former Rhodesian soldiers. The stadium was tear gassed, and Bob, still in a trance-like state, trying to sing, had to be led off the stage. But order returned, and Marley left Africa safely, ready for a sell-out tour of Europe.

The 1980 tour was to be Bob Marley's last and it rocked Europe. In the Tivoli Gardens in the Danish capital, Copenhagen, The Wailers broke Abba's and Bob Dylan's records for the highest attendance ever. They played from Berlin to Barcelona, from Dublin to Milan, breaking the attendance records of bands like the Beatles and the Rolling Stones wherever they went.

Good Rastaman

Bob Marley once said in an interview: "I see myself, maybe, as a good man. Me want to be a good man. ... I want to be a good Rasta man. Never die."

One day in September 1980, while jogging in Central Park with Allan Cole, Marley collapsed. He was immediately diagnosed as having cancer. The doctor told him he had only a few weeks to live.

There followed a time of painful treatment, hospitals, and a long journey home that he never finished. The cancer began to spread throughout his body. He was rushed by Concorde to a private clinic in Germany. There, the illness was temporarily driven back by a course of intensive treatment, but the cancer remained. Then, his condition worsened, and he began to make his way back to Jamaica. In Miami, nine months after he had collapsed, he could go no further, and he died on May 11, 1981, aged thirty-six, in the Cedars of Lebanon hospital.

On the day he died, Bob said to his son Ziggy: "The place where I am is beautiful, it's green and fresh, but when I look down on earth, there's darkness and doom, but just hold on, unite with people and with mother."

His last words to Rita on that sunny morning were "Rita, I'm not going anywhere, I not leaving you go nowhere, I'll be with you always."

Rita's feelings at the loss of Bob were greatly affected by her beliefs - the ones she and Bob shared. She explained them in this way: "Prophesy say when one man dies, the Lord rejoice, but when one is born, mourn

53

HON. ROBERT NESTA MARLEY O.M.

Above: The funeral service for Bob took place at 11a.m. on May 21, 1981. His coffin was placed on the stage of the National Arena in Kingston and draped with the Ethiopian flag.

Opposite: The roads from Kingston to Nine Miles were thickly lined with mourning Jamaicans waving flags, pictures of Bob and palm fronds.

because we don't know which spirit going into that flesh, into the mother's womb, so that is the time you must mourn and lament and hope that this is going to be a good one. But when one pass away you give thanks...I can imagine that Bob feel free."

They were not just brave words that Rita Marley spoke after Bob's death. The spirit of his funeral, his great send-off from earth, and the spirit he left behind, really did seem to be more of a spirit of rejoicing than one of gloom. While people everywhere reeled from the shock of his death, and Jamaica went into a period of national mourning, preparations were under way for an extraordinary farewell to the great man.

Unlike western funerals, which are dominated by black, Bob's funeral was a splash of brilliant greens and

reds. The Jamaican black, green and gold ran riot with the Rasta red, gold and green. Many people were dressed in pure white to mourn.

The ceremony took place in the Ethiopian Orthodox Church in Kingston. For ten days, multitudes of people filed past Marley's coffin to pay their last respects. On the day of his burial, the rituals performed went back to the roots of African civilization, to the earliest days of Ethiopia.

Frankincense and myrrh were burned. The coffin lay in state throughout the service, which - in a highly modern ritual - was beamed live by satellite all over the world. The service included scripture readings. Cedella, Rita and the I-Threes all wished their own heartfelt farewells. Ziggy and Stephen said goodbye to their father by dancing a jive on stage.

After the service, the coffin was carried along the winding road to his home village. The way was lined with people saying their last goodbyes. The journey was long and hard. Although many present were overcome by the loss, those closest to Bob seemed somehow buoyed up by the curious hope and conviction Rita expressed. Judy Mowatt, one of the I-Threes, shared this belief in new life, beyond our existence here on earth: "I know that I will see my brother again", she said.

Legend

At the time of his death, Marley's world album sales exceeded $190m. On May 11, 1982, the first anniversary of his death, the record company CBS brought out "Birth of a Legend, Parts 1 and 2", which were essentially Bob Marley and the Wailers' greatest hits. There were video releases and television promotions. But scarcely any mention was made of reggae as a music form. In 1983, two years after Bob's death, an album called "Confrontation" was released. It contained five tracks never before released in any form. A year later, Island Records released their "Legend" album and it was the company's biggest selling album in ten years.

By 1984, Bob Marley was a household name, a figure who beamed out from a million posters, and who was surrounded by an aura of nostalgia. It was as though his early death planed away the rough edges of his message - many people seemed to want to remember him only as the quiet, gentle singer of "One Love". But he left behind him a legacy that has turned into a multi-million dollar legal tangle.

Legacy

Bob Marley never made a will. Some say this was because he scorned red tape and had so little concern for possessions. His daughter, Cedella, has her own interpretation: "He didn't make a will because he was like all of us," she said in 1991. "He thought he was going to live forever."

The lack of a will meant that Bob Marley's estate, valued at $8 million at the time of his death and $30 million in 1991, went to his wife, Rita. Most of the value lay in unreleased music which would perpetuate the Bob Marley legend after his death. There were also businesses, properties and royalties from the published music.

"The fundamental elements of his philosophy were the self. He leaves behind a legacy of rhythm, good will and just plain love that can never die. The world needed Bob Marley more than he needed it."

Robert Santelli, from "The Aquarian National", 1981.

In the years following his death, the mothers of Marley's illegitimate children (the so-called "baby mothers") complained that they received no money for the upkeep of their children. Marley's mother, Cedella Booker, herself suffered the humiliation of being legally pronounced "a stranger to the estate". The former Wailers were given small amounts of money by Rita, along with a long, complex contract a lawyer had prepared, which left them feeling they had been cheated.

By 1986, the Marley estate had generated a number of law suits: ex-members of the Wailers and some of the baby-mothers were suing Rita, two of Bob's accountants and a former lawyer were being sued - one law suit alone cost $3.5m. The estate was in danger of being entirely used up on lawyer's fees.

It will come right

Sometimes, in the midst of all the legal wrangles and bitterness, it seems as though the music and message of Bob Marley has been obscured. He once answered a journalist's persistent questions about money with

Opposite and above: Bob Marley's image lives on, his music continues to inspire his listeners.
Top: Bob's mother, Cedella Booker, embraces the words "Bob Lives" outside his birthplace.

"Why you no check the heart that beat instead of the bank account?" And he is quoted as saying, "I know I was born with a price on my head."

As for the Marley family, they feel a mixture of sorrow and anger over this unresolved battle: "This family is recognized by millions of people worldwide," said Rita in interview. "We have something to stand for and we have always thought that there were more important things than money...It's a long game we're playing," she concluded staunchly, "and Jah will make it come right in the end."

Just the beginning

The end of Bob Marley's life marked the beginning of a legend. As always when a public figure dies, there was no shortage of tributes paid to Bob by those in the public eye themselves. Both Jamaica's political leaders were voluble in their praise of the national hero. Just a few weeks before his death Marley had been given the Jamaican Order of Merit.

"He was a genius. He's one of those extraordinary figures that...comes along perhaps once in a generation; who, starting with a folk art, a folk form, by some inner magic of commitment, sincerity of passion and of just skill, turns it into a part of the universal language of the arts of the world," the leader of the Jamaican People's National Party, Michael Manley, said of Bob.

Many other leaders, rock stars, reggae stars, and poets spoke publicly of their deep regard for Marley. While some saw him as great only in terms of music, most people recognized an extra dimension to the man's importance: they saw him as a spokesperson for the blacks of Jamaica and for the fight for their rights. Some people could see that Bob Marley "woke up" the oppressed people of the world; he had been told personally by people in Africa that when he sang, they felt as though he were talking directly to them.

It was this quality of universality that drew people together when they heard his music. It was a message of hope, comfort and anger. "Everything in life got it's purpose," he sang,

"Find it's reason in every season"
("Forever Loving Jah").

"If we come from a different planet, we could never come together. But we all come from the same father. That is why it is possible to come together."

Bob Marley, from the "Hotpress" article, 1978.

Important Dates

1496   The first white people land on Jamaica, home of the Arawak Indians.

1834   Black slavery ends in Jamaica.

1887   Marcus Garvey is born in St. Ann, Jamaica.

1914   Garvey sets up the Universal Negro Improvement Association (UNIA) with the aim of creating an independent nation for black people in Africa.

1922   Marcus Garvey is charged with fraud by the American government and is deported.

1930   Haile Selassie is crowned Emperor of Ethiopia.

1940   Marcus Garvey dies in London, England - a national hero of Jamaica.

1944   June 9: Captain Norval Marley marries Cedella Booker.

1946   Feb. 6: Robert Nesta Marley is born to Norval and Cedella Marley in the village of St. Ann, Jamaica.

1951   Bob's father takes the four-year-old to the Jamaican capital, Kingston, but Cedella fetches him back.

1955   Bob's father, Captain Norval Marley, dies.

1957   Bob, aged eleven, moves to Kingston.

1960   Bob, aged fifteen, finishes school and takes up welding. He also releases his first single, "Judge Not". His mother, Cedella, moves to America and is married to Edward Booker.

1964   Bob founds the Wailing Wailers with Bunny Livingston and Pete Tosh.

1966   Feb. 10: Bob Marley, aged twenty-one and Rita Anderson, aged nineteen, are married. Bob leaves for America the following day.

1967   Bob returns to Jamaica.

1968   Bob goes to Europe to record backing vocals on the American JAD label.

1971   The Wailing Wailers are signed to Island Records by Chris Blackwell.

1973   The Wailers' first album, "Catch a Fire", is released. The same year, they release their second album, "Burnin'."

1974   Pete Tosh and Bunny Livingston leave the band. It is renamed Bob Marley and the Wailers.

1975   Bob Marley's first solo album, "Natty Dread", is released. Emperor Haile Selassie is reported dead.

1976   The "Rastaman Vibration" album is released.
A state of emergency is declared in Jamaica in the lead-up to national elections. Bob Marley and the Wailers tour North America and Canada.
An attempt is made on Bob's life in Kingston and he leaves Jamaica.

1978   Bob Marley, aged thirty-two, returns to Jamaica for the One Love One Peace concert.

1979   Bob Marley and the Wailers' ninth album, "Survival", is released.
The band embarks on a world tour.

1980   The band goes on a second world tour, starting at the Zimbabwe independence celebrations.
        Marley's last album, "Uprising", is released.
        Sept. 21: Bob collapses while running in Central Park, New York and is diagnosed as having cancer.

1981   May 11: Bob Marley, aged thirty-six, dies.

1982   CBS release Bob Marley's greatest hits on "Birth of a Legend Parts 1 and 2".

1983   The posthumous album, "Confrontation", is released.

Recommended Listening

Concrete Jungle from the album, Catch a Fire, 1973
Get Up, Stand Up from Burnin', 1973
Could You Be Loved from Burnin', 1973
No Woman, No Cry from Natty Dread, 1974
Redemption Song from Uprising, 1980
Coming In From The Cold from Uprising, 1980

Glossary

Antiphony: The musical effect of an echo. One group sings a verse or phrase and it is repeated by an alternate group.

Babylon: According to the *Rastafari* religion, any evil force, place or person.

Bongo: A small, bucket-shaped drum played with the fingers and usually played in pairs. Also, an insulting term for black people in the West Indies.

Brams: Country dances in Jamaica.

Dread: The quality of Rude Boys and *Rastas,* a mixture of rebellion, righteous anger and determination.

Dreadlocks: The long, uncombed locks of matted hair worn by *Rastas* and many reggae fans. They are worn because of an instruction in the Bible not to cut the hair.

Emissary: Someone who is sent on an important mission.

Fife: A small flute, with no keys, similar to the piccolo. It is usually played in military bands.

Fretwork: The ridges of metal or ivory bars that are set across the fingerboard of a musical instrument such as a guitar or banjo. They mark the position of the different musical pitches.

Ghetto: An area of a city inhabited by a minority group.

Gospel: Black religious music. There are different types of gospel music some of which originated from traditional preaching, singing and shouting with some *jazz* and blues influences.

Guerrilla: An unofficial soldier, not normally attached to any government, who fights as part of an independent group.

Hausa: The language of the Negroid people of West Africa, widely used in Nigeria.

Jah: The *Rasta* word for God. It is abbreviated from *Jehovah.*

Jazz: A complex music form which has evolved over many years in the southern states of America and is derived from folk music and some slave music. New Orleans jazz is sometimes called Dixieland jazz and started evolving about 1910.

Jehovah: The personal name of God, said to have been revealed to Moses in the Old Testament of the Bible.

Judge Dread: A mythical figure in Jamaica who handed out strict judgments and sentences of suffering. The Jamaicans gave the whole system this persona, making it easier to understand.

King, Martin Luther: The American Baptist minister and civil-rights leader who campaigned peacefully against the segregation of Negroes in the southern states of America. He won the Nobel Peace Prize in 1964 and was assassinated in 1968.

Mento: Jamaican dance music that was popular in the early twentieth century. It usually has lots of *percussion* and guitars playing at the same time.

Percussion: The group of instruments that are played by striking or banging against each other.

Rasta: Short for Rastafarian, someone who belongs to the *Rastafari religion.*

Rastafari religion: The Jamaican religious movement that recognizes His Imperial *Haile Selassie* as the Black Messiah and believes in the return of all black people to Africa as their homeland.

Rhythm and Blues: African/American popular music mixing blues and *jazz* styles with a strong rhythm. It was the first black music to become popular with white people.

Selassie, Haile: Emperor of Ethiopia from 1939 to 1975.

Zion: A Biblical term meaning the promised land; for *Rastas* this means Africa.

Index